BRITISH MUSEUM

# Christmas Carols

BRITISH MUSEUM 𝕀𝕀𝕀𝕀𝕀 PRESS

# Contents

# ntroduction

THE CAROLS in this book are illustrated with festive greetings cards, mostly marking Christmas and New Year, from a collection built up by Queen Mary, the consort of King George V.

May of Teck, the future Queen Mary, started collecting cards as a young girl. She kept those that had been given to her, especially by her mother and Queen Victoria, and also those sent between other immediate relatives. Many cards afford a touching insight into the manner of greeting between members of the Royal Family, including 'Lilibet', the future Queen Elizabeth II. King George V's redundant stamp albums were later pressed into service by Queen Mary to accommodate all the cards that she had amassed.

Since 1947 the British Museum has been the custodian of these albums. Thirty-one in total, they contain a mixture of cards and other forms of greeting from 1872 to 1952. They include

some examples of the best, most expensive types of card produced during the period. This is an important collection not only because of its royal connections and the quality of often extraordinarily rare cards, some of which are unique handmade pieces, but because it also represents the development of the printing of ephemeral objects.

The collection is very strong on cards made in Germany, the leading country in the production of high-quality cards for an expanding international market. In an album featuring cards produced and sent between 1872 and 1893, there are sumptous examples of chromolithography in its heyday. Many are novelty cards, such as the one illustrated above. When closed, it bears the gilt inscription in German *Ich gratulire* on the front panel; when the panel is pulled down, a finely manufactured 'pop up' townscape appears.

The earliest images of New Year greeting held by the British Museum are two fifteenth-century German woodcuts. These prints are not from Queen Mary's albums, but are part of a separate holding that includes an example (from George Buday's renowned collection) of the famous first Christmas card, designed by J.C. Horsley for Sir Henry Cole in 1843. Horsley's card, which had been Cole's idea, was lithographed by Jobbins of Holborn, London. It represents a Pickwickian scene of seasonal merriment supported by more sober pictures of charitable acts. Even earlier, in 1840, R. Doyle had designed the first Christmas envelope, which was published by Fores of Piccadilly, London. The impetus for this activity and for the custom of sending greetings and then cards at Christmas and New Year was the introduction of the Penny Post in 1840. This made it possible to greet friends at various geographical distances for the same cost.

Many British manufacturers of early cards have survived into our own age. They include Goodall, Raphael Tuck, Marcus Ward and De La Rue, the latter being best known now for printing

bank notes. De La Rue were so prolific that they added a series number to each card design from the late 1870s.

Goodall produced the popular 'Voiced' cards in the 1870s. Two such cards, both patented in 1877, appear in Queen Mary's Collection and were sent to her as a child by her mother. The 'voiced' robin New Year card *(see page 47)* was sent in 1879. On the back is a small packet containing a 'squeaker', which emits a 'peep' when the robin's breast is pressed. The other card, dated New Year 1880, shows geese and a magpie *(see page 13)*. These Goodall cards, in their complete form, with their 'voices', are very rare survivals.

Famous designers worked for specialist publishers of Christmas and New Year cards. Marcus Ward published several of the delicate designs of Kate Greenaway in the 1870s *(see page 45)*.

Unseasonal flowers often figured on the Christmas and New Year cards, regularly using the Language of Flowers. The choice of flower needed to be made with great care: roses could be read as meaning pure and lovely, whereas a yellow chrysanthemum may imply love ignored.

The Fine Art card emerged in the late 1880s, being particularly developed in Berlin. An example collected by Queen Mary bears a photographic reproduction of Ittenbach's painting of the Christ Child; it was sent by Queen Victoria at Osborne to 'Louise' in 1889. The Castell Brothers in Bavaria specialized in producing chromolithographic copies of Old Master paintings for cards.

The cards reproduced in this book have been chosen to complement the carols they are paired with rather than to illustrate the true wealth and scope of Queen Mary's Collection. They do nonetheless offer a tantalizing glimpse at what the albums contain.

HILARY WILLIAMS

G . R .   W O O D W A R D   ( 1 8 4 8 – 1 9 3 4 )

# Ding Dong! Merrily on High

Ding-dong! merrily on high
In heav'n the bells are ringing:
Ding-dong! verily the sky
Is riv'n with angel singing.
*Gloria, Hosanna in excelsis!*

E'en so here below, below,
Let steeple bells be swungen,
And *io, io, io,*
By priest and people sungen.
*Gloria, Hosanna in excelsis!*

Pray you, dutifully prime
Your matin chime, ye ringers;
May you beautifully rime
Your evetime song, ye singers.
*Gloria, Hosanna in excelsis!*

# Christmas is Coming

CHRISTMAS IS COMING, the geese are getting fat,
　　Please to put a penny in the old man's hat.
If you haven't got a penny, a ha'p'ny'll do,
　　If you haven't got a ha'p'ny, a farthing'll do,
If you haven't got a farthing, God bless you!

A Happy New Year.

# Watts' Cradle Song

Hush! my dear, lie still and slumber;
Holy angels guard thy bed!
Heav'nly blessings without number
Gently falling on thy head.

Sleep, my babe; thy food and raiment,
House and home, thy friends provide;
All without thy care and payment,
All thy wants are well supplied.

How much better thou'rt attended
Than the Son of God could be
When from heaven he descended,
And became a child like thee.

Soft and easy is thy cradle;
Coarse and hard thy Saviour lay,
When his birth-place was a stable
And his softest bed was hay.

*Continued…*

Christmas blessings be thine

See the lovely babe addressing:
Lovely infant, how he smiled!
When he wept, the mother's blessing
Soothed and hushed the holy child.

>Lo, he slumbers in his manger,
>Where the horned oxen fed;
>Peace, my darling! here's no danger;
>Here's no ox anear thy bed.

May'st thou live to know and fear him,
Trust and love him all thy days:
Then go dwell for ever near him,
See his face and sing his praise.

JAMES MONTGOMERY (1771–1854)

# Angels, from the Realms of Glory

ANGELS, from the realms of glory,
Wing your flight o'er all the earth;
Ye, who sang creation's story,
Now proclaim Messiah's birth:

> *Gloria in excelsis Deo,*
> *Gloria in excelsis Deo!*

Shepherds, in the field abiding,
Watching o'er your flocks by night,
God with man is now residing,
Yonder shines the infant light:

> *Gloria, etc.*

Sages, leave your contemplations;
Brighter visions beam afar;
Seek the great desire of nations;
Ye have seen his natal star:

> *Gloria, etc.*

Saints before the altar bending,
Watching long in hope and fear,
Suddenly the Lord, descending,
In his temple shall appear:

> *Gloria, etc.*

Though an infant now we view him,
He shall fill his Father's throne,
Gather all the nations to him;
Ev'ry knee shall then bow down:

> *Gloria, etc.*

J O H N   H E N R Y   H O P K I N S   ( 1 8 2 0 – 9 1 )

# We Three Kings of Orient Are

WE THREE kings of Orient are;
Bearing gifts we traverse afar
Field and fountain, moor and mountain,
Following yonder star:

> *O star of wonder, star of night,*
> *Star with royal beauty bright,*
> *Westward leading, still proceeding,*
> *Guide us to thy perfect light.*

**Melchior:**
Born a king on Bethlehem plain,
Gold I bring, to crown him again,
King for ever, ceasing never,
Over us all to reign:

> *O star of wonder, etc.*

*Continued…*

BOUASSE-LEBEL & FILS & MASSIN          M. 126          29, RUE St SULPICE, PARIS.

THE THREE GIFTS:
THE GOLD OF LOVE, THE MYRRH OF SELF-DENIAL,
AND THE INCENSE OF PRAYER.

**Caspar:**

Frankincense to offer have I,

Incense owns a deity nigh;

Prayer and praising, all men raising,

Worship him, God most high:

*O star of wonder, etc.*

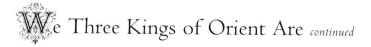

**Balthazar:**

Myrrh is mine; its bitter perfume

Breathes a life of gathering gloom;

Sorrowing, sighing, bleeding, dying,

Sealed in the stone-cold tomb:

**All:**

Glorious now, behold him arise,

King and God and sacrifice,

Heav'n sings alleluia,

Alleluia the earth replies:

*O star of wonder, etc.*

*O star of wonder, etc.*

# In the Bleak Midwinter

IN THE BLEAK midwinter
Frosty wind made moan,
Earth stood hard as iron,
Water like a stone;
Snow has fallen, snow on snow,
Snow on snow,
In the bleak midwinter,
Long ago.

Our God, Heav'n cannot hold him
Nor earth sustain;
Heav'n and earth shall flee away
When he comes to reign:
In the bleak midwinter
A stable place sufficed
The Lord God Almighty
Jesus Christ.

*Continued…*

*A glad New Year to you.*

Enough for him, whom cherubim
Worship night and day,
A breastful of milk,
And a mangerful of hay;
Enough for him, whom angels
Fall down before,
The ox and ass and camel
Which adore.

Angels and archangels
May have gathered there,
Cherubim and seraphim
Thronged the air;
But only his mother
In her maiden bliss
Worshipped the Beloved
With a kiss.

What can I give him,
Poor as I am?
If I were a shepherd
I would bring a lamb;
If I were a wise man
I would do my part,
Yet what I can I give him,
Give my heart.

*Christmas Blessings be yours*
*dear May, from y.r very affectionate aunt*
*Beatrice*

ANONYMOUS

# Away in a Manger

AWAY IN A MANGER, no crib for a bed,
The little Lord Jesus laid down his sweet head;
The stars in the bright sky look'd down where he lay,
The little Lord Jesus asleep on the hay.

The cattle are lowing, the baby awakes,
But little lord Jesus no crying he makes.
I love thee, Lord Jesus! Look down from the sky,
And stay by my side until morning is nigh.

Be near me, Lord Jesus; I ask thee to stay
Close by me for ever, and love me, I pray.
Bless all the dear children in thy tender care,
And fit us for heaven, to live with thee there.

"Unto you is born a Saviour."

CHARLES WESLEY (1707–88) AND OTHERS

# Hark! The Herald Angels Sing

Hark! the herald angels sing,
Glory to the new-born King;
Peace on earth and mercy mild,
God and sinners reconciled:
Joyful all ye nations rise,
Join the triumph of the skies;
With th'angelic host proclaim,
Christ is born in Bethlehem.

*Hark! the herald angels sing,*
*Glory to the new-born King.*

Christ, by highest heav'n adored,
Christ, the everlasting Lord,
Late in time behold him come,
Offspring of a virgin's womb.
Veiled in flesh the Godhead see,
Hail, th'incarnate Deity!
Pleas'd as man with man to dwell,
Jesus, our Emmanuel.

*Hark! etc.*

Hail, the heav'n-born Prince of Peace!
Hail, the Sun of Righteousness!
Light and life to all he brings,
Ris'n with healing in his wings;
Mild he lays his glory by,
Born that man no more may die,
Born to raise the sons of earth,
Born to give them second birth.

*Hark! etc.*

Gli angioli del GOZZOLI
vi portino i miei auguri

Edmund H. Sears (1810–76)

# It Came Upon the Midnight Clear

It CAME UPON the midnight clear,
    That glorious song of old,
From angels bending near the earth
    To touch their harps of gold:
'Peace on the earth, goodwill to men,
    From heav'n's all-gracious King!'
The world in solemn stillness lay
    To hear the angels sing.

Still through the cloven skies they come,
    With peaceful wings unfurled;
And still their heav'nly music floats
    O'er all the weary world;
Above its sad and lowly plains
    They bend on hov'ring wing;
And ever o'er its Babel sounds
    The blessed angels sing.

Yet with the woes of sin and strife
    The world has suffered long;
Beneath the angel strain have rolled
    Two thousand years of wrong;
And man, at war with man, hears not
    The love song which they bring:
O hush the noise, ye men of strife,
    And hear the angels sing!

For lo! the days are hast'ning on,
    By prophet bards foretold,
When, with the ever-circling years,
    Comes round the age of gold;
When peace shall over all the earth
    Its ancient splendours fling,
And the whole world give back the song
    Which now the angels sing.

# The First Nowell

THE FIRST NOWELL the angel did say,
Was to certain poor shepherds in fields as they lay;
In fields where they lay keeping their sheep,
On a cold winter's night that was so deep.

*Nowell, Nowell, Nowell, Nowell,*
*Born is the King of Israel!*

They looked up and saw a star,
Shining in the east, beyond them far;
And to the earth it gave great light,
And so it continued both day and night.

*Nowell, etc.*

And by the light of that same star,
Three wise men came from country far;
To see for a king was their intent,
And to follow the star wherever it went.

*Nowell, etc.*

This star drew nigh to the northwest,
O'er Bethlehem it took its rest,
And there it did both stop and stay
Right over the place where Jesus lay.

*Nowell, etc.*

Then entered in those wise men three,
Full rev'rently upon their knee,
And offer'd there, in his presence,
Their gold, and myrrh, and frankincense.

*Nowell, etc.*

Then let us all with one accord
Sing praises to our heav'nly Lord,
That hath made heav'n and earth of naught,
And with his blood mankind hath bought.

*Nowell, etc.*

Heaven bless thee, brightening, every YEAR!

# 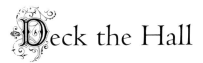eck the Hall

Deck the Hall with boughs of holly,
*Fa la la la la, la la la la,*
'Tis the season to be jolly,
*Fa la la la, la la la la,*
Don we now our gay apparel,
*Fa la la, la la la, la la la,*
Troll the ancient yuletide carol,
*Fa la la, la la la la la.*

See the blazing yule before us,
*Fa la la la la, la la la la,*
Strike the harp and join the chorus,
*Fa la la la, la la la la,*
Follow me in a merry measure,
*Fa la la, la la la, la la la,*
While I tell of yuletide treasure,
*Fa la la, la la la la la.*

Fast away the old year passes,
*Fa la la la la, la la la la,*
Hail the new, ye lads and lasses,
*Fa la la la, la la la la,*
Sing we joyous all together,
*Fa la la, la la la, la la la,*
Heedless of the wind and weather,
*Fa la la, la la la la la.*

*OLD AND YOUNG THEN JOIN IN PLAY.*

*TO GLADDEN THIS OUR NEW YEAR'S DAY*

Little Town of Bethlehem

O LITTLE TOWN of Bethlehem,
How still we see thee lie!
Above thy deep and dreamless sleep
The silent stars go by.
Yet in thy dark streets shineth
The everlasting light;
The hopes and fears of all the years
Are met in thee tonight.

O morning stars, together
Proclaim the holy birth,
And praises sing to God the King,
And peace to men on earth;
For Christ is born of Mary;
And gather'd all above,
While mortals sleep, the angels keep
Their watch of wond'ring love.

How silently, how silently,
The wondrous gift is giv'n!
So God imparts to human hearts
The blessings of his heav'n.
No ear may hear his coming;
But in this world of sin,
Where meek souls will receive him, still
The dear Christ enters in.

O holy Child of Bethlehem,
Descends to us, we pray;
Cast out our sin and enter in,
Be born in us today.
We hear the Christmas angels
The great glad tidings tell:
O come to us, abide with us,
Our Lord Emmanuel.

Hail·Mary's
Little·One·Hail!
God's·Eternal·Son!

Sweet·Babe·of·Bethlehem

Faber

# Once in Royal David's City

Once in royal David's city
Stood a lowly cattle shed,
Where a mother laid her baby
In a manger for his bed;
Mary was the mother mild,
Jesus Christ her little child.

He came down to earth from heaven,
Who is God and Lord of all,
And his shelter was a stable,
And his cradle was a stall;
With the poor and mean and lowly,
Lived on earth our Saviour holy.

And through all his wondrous childhood
He would honour and obey,
Love and watch the lowly maiden,
In whose gentle arms he lay;
Christian children all must be
Mild, obedient, good as he.

*Continued…*

May all CHRISTMAS blessings be thine.

For he is our childhood's pattern,
Day by day like us he grew,
He was little, weak and helpless,
Tears and smiles like us he knew;
And he feeleth for our sadness,
And he shareth in our gladness.

And our eyes at last shall see him,
Through his own redeeming love,
For that child so dear and gentle
Is our Lord in heaven above;
And he leads his children on
To the place where he is gone.

Not in that poor lowly stable,
With the oxen standing by,
We shall see him; but in heaven,
Set at God's right hand on high;
When like stars his children crowned
All in white shall wait around.

# Going to the Party

Overcoats and wrappers
Furs and muffatees
Hands deep down in pockets
Cosy as you please
Little lads and lassies
Trotting through the snow
Tell us where you're going
We should like to know
To a Christmas Party
We are on our way
O such cakes and crackers
O such games of play
Now goodbye we cannot any longer wait
Or I do assure you we shall all be late.

TRADITIONAL

# Goodbye

Gᴏᴅ ʙʟᴇss the master of this house,
The mistress also,
And all the little children
That round the table go.

> *Love and joy come to you,*
> *And to you your wassail,*
> *Love and joy come to too,*
> *And God bless you, and send you*
> *A happy New Year.*

> And all your kin and kinsfolk,
> That dwell both far and near:
> I wish you a merry Christmas,
> And a happy New Year.

> *Love and joy, etc*

Wishing you A Happy New Year

© 1998 The Trustees of the British Museum

Introduction by Hilary Williams

*Ding Dong! Merrily on High* reproduced by permission of SPCK

First published in 1998 by British Museum Press

A division of the British Museum Company Ltd

46 Bloomsbury Street, London WC1B 3QQ

A catalogue record for this book is available from
the British Library

ISBN 0 7141 2707 8

Designed by

THE BRIDGEWATER BOOK COMPANY

Printed in Slovenia by Korotan

Acknowledgements

The Publishers would like to thank Hilary Williams,
Education Service, British Museum; Ivor Kerslake and
William Lewis, Photographic Service, British Museum;
the Department of Prints and Drawings, British Museum;
and the Royal Library, Windsor Castle.